DATE DUE

FEB 13 '90			

WORLD IN VIEW
ENGLAND
Mary Peplow & Debra Shipley

STECK-VAUGHN
LIBRARY
Austin, Texas

914.2
Pep

Published in the United States in 1990 by Steck-Vaughn
Co., Austin, Texas, a subsidiary of National Education
Corporation.

First published 1989 by
Macmillan Children's Books
A division of
MACMILLAN PUBLISHERS LTD

Designed by Julian Holland
Picture research by Faith Perkins

Library of Congress Cataloging-in-Publication Data

Peplow. Mary.
    England/Mary Peplow & Debra Shipley.
       p. cm.—(World in view)
    "First published 1989 by Macmillan Children's Books."
    Summary: A general description of England,
including history, daily life, agriculture, industry and
trade, communications, education, health and welfare
systems, leisure activities, and cultural life.
    ISBN 0-8114-2428-6
    1. England—Juvenile literature.   [1. England.]
I. Shipley, Debra. II. Title. III. Series.   89.21786
DA27.5. P46   1990   CIP
942—dc20   AC

Printed and bound in the United States.
1 2 3 4 5 6 7 8 9 0 LB 94 93 92 91 90

Photographic credits
Cover: Barry Waddams, title page: Robert Harding Photograph Library, 8 Robert Harding
Photograph Library, 9 Margaret Sinclair, 10 Robert Harding Photograph Library, 12/13 Robert
Harding Photograph Library, 13 NHPA Stephen Dalton, 16 Michael Holford Archit, 17 Mary
Evans Picture Library, 21 Bridgeman Art library, 26 Mary Evans Picture Library, 28 Rex
Features, 29 Robert Harding Photograph Library, 31 Camera Press, 33 Robert Harding
Photograph Library, 38 Topham, 40 Topham, 41 J. Allan Cash, 44 Robert Harding Photograph
Library, 49 Science Photo Library, 51 J. Cash, 52 Robert Harding Photograph Library, 53 Acton
Scott Working Museum Shropshire, 55 Robert Harding Photograph Library, 56 Robert
Harding Photograph Library, 57 Peter Newark Historical Pictures, 58 J. Allan Cash, 61 Robert
Harding Photograph Library, 64 Sally & Richard Greenhill, 65 Sally & Richard Greenhill, 67
Sally & Richard Greenhill, 69 Picturepoint, 72 Sally & Richard Greenhill, 74 Robert Harding
Photograph Library, 77 J. Allan Cash, 78 Sally & Richard Greenhill, 80 Robert Harding
Photograph Library, 84 Topham, 88 Reg Wilson, 91 Bridgman Art Library, Tate Gallery,
London, 92 J. Allan Cash.

Contents

SCOTLAND

0   50   100 Mi

0   50   100   150 Km.

R. Tyne

Newcastle-upon-Tyne

Carlisle

Durham

Hartlepool

NORTH SEA

Lake District

R. Tees

Stockton

Darlington

▲ *Scafell Pike 978m*

Vale of York

Yorkshire Moors

T h e   P e n n i n e s

ISLE OF MAN

Lancaster

York

IRISH SEA

Blackpool

R. Ribble

Leeds

Selby

R. Humber

Bradford

Grimsby

Salford

Manchester

Liverpool

R. Mersey

Sheffield

Peak District

Lincoln Wolds

Skegness

Vale of Trent

R. Trent

E N G L A N D

R. Severn

Midlands

Norwich

R. Nerne

W A L E S

Birmingham

The Fens

East Anglia

Vale of Evesham

Rugby

Great Ouse

Cambridge

R. Avon

Stratford-on-Avon

Ipswich

Cotswold Hills

Oxford

Chiltern Hills

Southend

R. Thames

London

Bristol

Bristol Channel

Bath

North Downs

Canterbury

Weston-super-Mare

Mendip Hills

Salisbury Plain

South Downs

Tunbridge Wells

The Weald

Dover

Exmoor

Southampton

Portsmouth

Brighton

Axminster

Exeter

Dartmoor

Plymouth

Land's End

E N G L I S H   C H A N N E L

Cross of St George   Union Flag

1 Introducing England

On a map of the world, you will find the British Isles to the northwest of Europe, and England is the main country in those islands. Although both small and insignificant, the British Isles have had a place in history and in world affairs that is out of all proportion to their size.

England has a total area of 53,330 square miles. On the north side, it is joined to Scotland, and the west is bordered by Wales, the Irish Sea, and the Atlantic Ocean. To the east is the North Sea, and to the south the English Channel, which separates England from France and the rest of Europe. The country is divided into areas called counties for official purposes such as local education.

Around the coast
The seas around England's coast are fairly shallow and provide good fishing grounds. The coastline itself is 2,000 miles long and is very varied, with both bays and cliffs. Some beaches are pebbled, others have golden sand. Popular seaside resorts have grown up along many of the beaches. Nowhere in England is more than 75 miles from the sea.

Ports are to be found at the mouths of larger rivers. In the north of England, Liverpool, at the mouth of the Mersey River, is an important port. In the south, Southampton can be visited by the world's largest ocean liners.

Inland, England is mainly a lowland country, mostly less than 1,000 feet above sea level. There

ENGLAND

1. Northumberland
2. Tyne and Wear
3. Cleveland
4. Durham
5. Cumbria
6. North Yorkshire
7. Lancashire
8. Merseyside
9. Greater Manchester
10. West Yorkshire
11. South Yorkshire
12. Humberside
13. Lincolnshire
14. Nottinghamshire
15. Derbyshire
16. Cheshire
17. Staffordshire
18. Salop
19. Hereford and Worcester
20. West Midlands
21. Warwickshire
22. Leicestershire
23. Northamptonshire
24. Bedfordshire
25. Cambridgeshire
26. Norfolk
27. Suffolk
28. Essex
29. Greater London
30. Hertfordshire
31. Buckinghamshire
32. Oxfordshire
33. Gloucestershire
34. Avon
35. Wittshire
36. Berkshire
37. Surrey
38. Kent
39. East Sussex
40. West Sussex
41. Hampshire
42. Isle of Wight
43. Dorset
44. Somerset
45. Devon
46. Cornwall and the
    Isles of Scilly

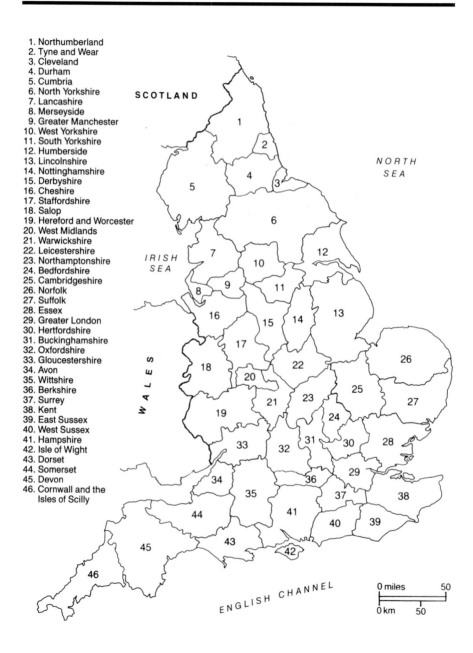

are some highland areas in the north, such as the Cumbrian mountains which include England's highest peak, Scafell Pike, at 3,210 feet. Toward the center and south of England, however, the land becomes gradually flatter, with ranges of gentle rounded hills, like the Cotswolds, rather than mountains.

The seasons
The temperature in England is generally mild, though it does tend to be warmer in the south than in the north. In both the north and the south of England, and at all times of the year, there is a good deal of rain and nearly everyone uses an umbrella. The rain is not, however, sufficient to prevent drought from time to time.

In the winter months of December, January, and February, the temperature can go below 4°F. During these months, snow may fall and occasionally roads are blocked by drifts. March, April, and May are the months of spring, when the trees come into leaf and bulbs push shoots up through the earth. The first bulb to flower is usually the white snowdrop, which can often be spotted growing wild in woodland areas and along hedgerows. In England, the flower most associated with spring is the yellow daffodil, which can be seen growing wild and in gardens.

June, July, and August are the summer months, when the days are longest and hottest. Most people take their summer vacations at this time. Autumn comes in September, October, and November, when the leaves on the trees begin to change from green to yellow, orange, and brown.

During the autumn the last of the crops are

Beech woods are common in many parts of England. These magnificent trees grow tall and straight but their leafy cover shields the ground in high summer. Very little grows beneath them and in the autumn the ground is covered in russet leaves. However, the bare branches of winter months allow carpets of spring flowers, like these bluebells, to spread everywhere.

harvested, and birds and animals prepare for the winter. Many birds escape the cold English winter by flying to hotter countries in Africa. There are many birds that spend the winter months in England, however. One of these, the robin, is easily recognized by its bright red breast. It can be seen in gardens, in the country and in towns.

Town and country

There are about 47 million people living in England. London, which is the capital of the United Kingdom (England, Scotland, Wales, and Northern Ireland) has a population of about

8

seven million. Four out of every five people in England live in cities or towns.

In the country areas of England, people sometimes live in isolated farms, surrounded by fields and open land. Where there are two or three farms and houses built near one another, this is known as a hamlet. If there are a number of houses spread along several roads or lanes with perhaps a shop and a church, this is called a village. One example of a village is Kilmington in south Devon, which has a population of several hundred, a small church, and a butcher's shop. For other shopping the villagers must travel to the market town of Axminster or go to the city of Exeter, which is 20 miles away.

Dartmoor, one of England's best-known large

Most people in England live in towns or cities, but many of these towns are quite small. Some people prefer to live in towns around the edge of larger cities, where they feel life is not so busy and the community is more friendly. This street and market in Waltham Abbey still gives the impression of a small town, but in recent years it has become incorporated within the boundaries of Greater London.

There are several large cities in England with populations of over half a million, of which London is the largest. The centers of most of these cities are taken up by commerce and there are many offices. These people in the City of London are commuters crossing the Thames River on their way home from work. Nearly all commuters in London live some distance from their work and come into the city by train, bus, or car.

areas of countryside, is near Exeter. It is a fairly high, flat piece of land in the south of England made up of granite rock covered in poor scrub-like grass. Since it is unsuitable for growing

The currency is based on the unit of the pound sterling. This is symbolized by £. The pound is divided into 100 pence. Combinations of pence are available in coins, 1p, 2p, 5p, 10p, 20p, 50p and £1. The 20p and 50p are unusual in that they are heptagonal, or seven sided. Decimalization which divided the pound into units of 100 was only introduced in 1971. The pound sterling is an important currency in the international money market.

England has two flags that may be used: the red cross of St. George on a white background and the Union flag. St. George is the patron saint of England and this flag is often flown on holidays and special occasions. The Union flag or Union Jack, as it is often called, is the most widely recognized flag. It was first introduced in 1606 after the union of England and Scotland. At this time, it bore the cross of St. George and the cross of St. Andrew, which is a white diagonal cross on blue. After 1801, Ireland joined the union and the red diagonal cross on a white background was added. The words Union Jack should really only be applied when the flag is flying at the bow or stern of a Royal ship.

crops, this wild expanse is grazed by sheep and wild ponies. In contrast, the Fenland area in the east of England was once marshland. Through skillful drainage, the Fens have now become one of the most fertile parts of the country.

Animal and plant life

The geography of England is immensely varied. There is the rugged scenery of the Lake District and the Yorkshire Moors in the north, and the gentle beauty of counties such as Kent, some-times called the Garden of England, in the south. There is so much variety that many kinds of animals and plants thrive. Woodlands may contain trees such as oak, beech, birch, sycamore, and pine, and about 25,000 different types of animals are known to exist in England. Although 22,000 of those are insects, you may see larger

Although England is very densely populated there is still plenty of open countryside. This wintery view over Gurbar Edge in Derbyshire shows a small village in the countryside. Many of the people in the village work on the surrounding land. Others may work in a nearby town but prefer to live in the peace of the country.

mammals such as foxes and deer in the wild, as well as rabbits, hares, and squirrels. Foxes are now also making their homes within a few miles of the centers of big cities. There are very few snakes. Only one is poisonous: the adder, easily recognized by the V design on its back.

As cities have spread over
the countryside some of the
wildlife has learned to
adapt to urban living.
Foxes are now common in
several large cities, such as
Bristol. They live by
scavaging off the contents
of garbage cans. The
contents of this garbage
can show a typical example
of waste from an English
household.

13

2 England Through the Centuries

Two thousand years ago England was inhabited by people known as the Celts. The land was divided into small kingdoms each ruled by a royal house, some of whom even had their own coins. At one point the small kingdoms united to fight their common enemy when the Romans invaded the country in the first century A.D. The Romans then ruled much of England for around 300 years, but by the fifth century A.D. they had to withdraw, to help defend Rome.

England continued to be divided into small kingdoms until the ninth century. At that time Egbert, King of Wessex, became the very first king to rule all of England, although he did not call himself king of England.

Father of the English navy

The king best remembered from the ninth century is Alfred the Great. He not only started the English navy, he also compiled a code of laws, and established monasteries as centers of worship and learning. He was a warrior king as well, and fought many battles against Danish invaders.

The eleventh century brought a dramatic change to the English way of life. William, Duke of Normandy in France, thought the English throne should be his by right, and wanted to add England to his domains. He fought King Harold of England at the Battle of Hastings in 1066. He won the battle and Harold was killed. Later, on

Christmas Day, William was crowned King of England. He is known as William the Conqueror.

Domesday Book

William set about building cathedrals and castles. He also had a survey made of England's wealth in terms of land, animals, crops, and people. This was recorded in great detail in what is known as the Domesday Book.

After William's death, the throne of England passed to his son William Rufus who built a line of castles along the border of Wales. He was followed by his brother Henry I. Henry had wanted his daughter Matilda to succeed him, but at that time a woman was not allowed to rule. Instead, William of Normandy's grandson, Stephen of Blois, was appointed.

Matilda then invaded England, demanding her rightful crown, and civil war broke out. Stephen and Matilda eventually agreed that Stephen would remain king but that on his death Matilda's son Henry would inherit the throne.

Thomas Becket

Once crowned, Henry II restored law and order. However, he is remembered mainly in connection with the murder of Thomas Becket, Archbishop of Canterbury. The church in England at that time was both rich and powerful. Henry II decided to reform it, taking over some of the powers himself. He was opposed by Thomas Becket, and this made Henry so angry that one day he exclaimed, "Who will rid me of this turbulent priest?" Four of Henry's knights heard him and killed Thomas Becket in Canterbury Cathedral. The Pope made

This magnificent cathedral at Canterbury was built between the eleventh and the fifteenth centuries when the Church was very rich and powerful. Stonemasons may have spent their entire lives working on the intricate carvings. It was here that St. Thomas Becket was murdered by the king's knights in 1170. The Archbishop of Canterbury is the chief bishop, or Primate of All England.

Becket a saint, and his tomb became a place of pilgrimage.

Henry II was followed by his sons Richard and John. Richard took vows as a Crusader and went to fight in Jerusalem. The Crusaders were Christians who were fighting to make it possible once more for pilgrims to visit the Holy Sepulcher at Jerusalem. It had been taken over by the Muslims, followers of the Islam religion. Richard succeeded in this aim, and fought so bravely that he was known as Richard the Lion-Heart. Unfortunately, while he was away fighting he could not rule England well at the same time. His brother John ruled in his stead and became hated as a tyrant by the people of England.

The Wicked King

When John became king on his brother's death, he was known as the Wicked King. John demanded high taxes and imposed cruel punishments on his enemies. He was such a bad king that a group of powerful barons banded together to make him govern properly. King John was forced to meet the barons at Runnymede, where he was made to sign the Magna Carta. This great charter set out the rules that were to form the basis for the parliament which operates in England today.

When John died in 1216 his young son Henry succeeded him. Henry III was no better a king

In this old illustration, King John is seen signing the Magna Carta, which was to lay down the rules for governing England for many centuries. The Magna Carta was upheld in the seventeenth century as still being a statement of civil rights and a control on the power of the king. Original copies of the Charter are in the British Library and in Salisbury and Lincoln Cathedrals.

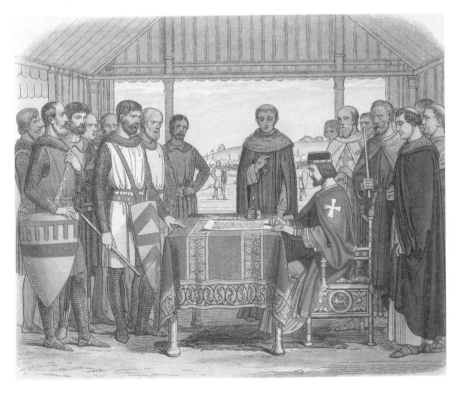

than his father and in 1258 civil war broke out again, lasting for most of his reign. His eldest son Edward I was crowned king on Henry III's death. During his reign, Edward added Wales to the English crown. He also conquered Scotland and took the coronation Stone of Scone to London. The Scots, however, continued to rebel. In 1307, Edward died on his way north to put down their rebellion and reconquer Scotland.

Edward II was born in Wales and in 1301 became the first prince to hold the title of Prince of Wales. He succeeded to the throne on his father's death, but was very unpopular. The barons tried to reduce his powers, and during his reign it became law that parliaments should be held at least once a year. In 1327 he was forced to give up the crown, that is, to abdicate, to his young son who became Edward III.

The Hundred Years' War

During Edward III's reign, the war with France known as the Hundred Years' War began. The English kings already owned a large part of France through inheritance; now Edward wanted the rest. The English fought many successful battles on French soil, sometimes led by Edward's son who was known as the Black Prince. One lasting effect of this war was that the English language replaced Norman French as the official language of England.

When the Black Prince's son Richard II took the throne in 1377, the ordinary people of England were beginning to desire a better life. Most importantly, working people demanded higher wages and the freedom to work wherever they wanted to, rather than for the nobles who owned the land they lived on. When a poll tax (that is, a payment of an equal amount from every single person) was demanded to pay for the continuing war with France, the peasants revolted. Richard told them that their demands would be met, but he did not keep his promises. In 1399 Richard was persuaded to abdicate, and Henry Bolingbroke came to the throne as King Henry IV. Henry was the son of John of Gaunt, the fourth son of Edward III. He took his surname from the place where he was born, Bolingbroke in Lincolnshire.

Henry V
Henry IV's claim to the throne was not a strong one, although he had been chosen by parliament to take Richard II's place. His eldest son, however, succeeded him as Henry V. The great task Henry V set himself during his reign was the conquest of France, and he almost achieved this. He had only one son, who came to the throne as Henry VI on the death of his father in 1422. However, Henry VI was only one year old when he succeeded, so the Duke of Gloucester was appointed as Protector of the country and shared power with a council until the young king was crowned in 1429.

The Wars of the Roses
The crown, however, was not secure because other descendants of Edward III had always had more right to it. They had split to form two royal households, the House of York whose emblem was a white rose and the House of Lancaster whose emblem was a red rose. The struggle

19

between these two royal houses broke into open warfare in 1455. This became known as the Wars of the Roses and lasted for 30 years. Henry VI belonged to the House of Lancaster and in 1461 he was deposed (that is, put off the throne) by the House of York, and Edward IV was declared king. When Edward died 22 years later, in 1483, his son Edward V reigned for just 75 days before he too died. Then Richard III, younger brother of Edward IV, was crowned king.

When Richard III was killed in 1485 at the Battle of Bosworth, the last major battle of the Wars of the Roses, Henry Tudor claimed the throne. His mother was a great grand-daughter of John of Gaunt, son of Edward III, and he was in the direct Lancastrian line of descent. Parliament agreed to recognize his claim and he became Henry VII. The fighting between the royal households was brought to an end when he married Princess Elizabeth of York, the daughter of Edward IV. By his marriage Henry merged the red and white roses, creating the united Tudor rose.

Henry VIII
Henry VII died in 1509, and was succeeded by his only surviving son, who was again called Henry. Henry VIII is one of the best known kings in English history and is important because he was responsible for the break of the English church from the authority of the Pope in Rome. Henry declared himself head of the Church of England. He was also the first English ruler to be called king of Ireland.

Henry desperately wanted a son to succeed him. When his first wife, Katherine of Aragon,

This picture shows Queen Elizabeth I at the height of her powers. She followed her father, Henry VIII, in making England one of the richest nations in the world. Her clothes are embroidered in gold thread and covered in jewels to show her immense wealth. In the background on the right, the English fleet is portrayed sailing out to meet the Spanish Armada.

produced only a daughter, he divorced her and married again. Henry had six wives in all in the attempt to produce a son. However, the only son born to him was the sickly Edward VI, son of Jane Seymour, who reigned for a short six years after his father died in 1547.

Lady Jane Grey, who was related to the younger sister of Henry VIII, was then queen for nine days before Mary, daughter of Henry VIII claimed the throne. Lady Jane Grey was beheaded the following year.

Two queens—Mary and Elizabeth

Queen Mary was not a follower of the Church of England. She was a follower of the Church of Rome and she was determined to make England once again a Catholic country. To this end she decided to marry her cousin Philip who was Roman Catholic and heir to the Spanish throne. Mary believed so strongly in the rightness of her cause that she also burned at the stake some 300 men and women who refused to change back to the Catholic faith. Both her marriage and her actions made her very unpopular.

After a struggle with her half-sister, Elizabeth, Mary was interred in the Tower of London and finally beheaded. Elizabeth came to the throne as Elizabeth I in 1558. Elizabeth was clever and well educated. She spoke many different languages and loved art. She wrote poetry and played music. Queen Elizabeth never married; instead she devoted herself to ruling England. A major threat to England at this time was Mary's husband, Philip II of Spain, who wanted to make England part of his empire. In 1588 Philip sent his fleet, now known as the Spanish Armada, to attack England. The Armada was defeated and Elizabeth continued to rule until her death in 1603.

Civil War

As Queen Elizabeth had no heir, the next in line for the throne was King James VI of Scotland, whose great-grandmother had been the daughter of Henry VII. He was crowned James I of England, and although he was at first popular, he made himself disliked by his attitude to parliament. James believed in the divine right of kings; that is, he thought his right to govern came directly from God. He was not ready therefore to listen to advice from a people's parliament. His son Charles I, who succeeded him in 1625, had similar views. Charles dissolved three parliaments in the first four years that he reigned. After that he ruled for nine years without a parliament, and this eventually led to civil war.

The Great Civil War, as it became known, lasted from 1642 until 1646. It was fought between the Roundheads, who were the parliamentary soldiers led by Oliver Cromwell, and the Cavaliers who were King Charles's supporters. Cromwell won, and Charles I was beheaded.

The Great Plague and the Great Fire of London

In the 1660s, London was a dirty, overcrowded place with timber houses packed tightly together. There was no sanitation and sewage flowed into pits beneath the buildings or down channels in the center of the streets. In these conditions rats flourished, and in 1665 the rats brought the bubonic plague which spread through London like wildfire. From 1665 to 1666 the Great Plague killed about 70,000 people. Then on September 2, 1666, the Great Fire of London started in a bakery in Pudding Lane. It burned for five days, demolishing 13,200 houses, St. Paul's Cathedral, 89 parish churches, and many public buildings; 200,000 people were made homeless. The damage was very costly but enabled London to be rebuilt in a new, more spacious style. The new St. Paul's Cathedral was designed by Christopher Wren, one of the leading architects of the seventeenth century.

From 1649 to 1659 England was called a Commonwealth. It was ruled first by Oliver Cromwell as Lord Protector and then by his son Richard.

The Restoration

In 1660 the monarchy was restored and Charles I's son was brought back from France, where he had fled for safety. He was crowned King Charles II in 1661. Charles's was an eventful reign. Seventy thousand people died from the Great Plague in 1665 and in the following year over 13,000 houses and churches were destroyed in the Great Fire of London. There were on the other hand scientific advances such as the building of Greenwich Observatory and Isaac Newton's discovery of the law of gravity.

Charles II arranged a marriage between his brother's daughter Mary and William, Prince of Orange, who were later appointed by parliament to the throne as joint monarchs in 1689. By that time Mary's father James II, who had succeeded Charles II, had been deposed because he wanted to make England a Catholic country once more.

William and Mary had no heir, so the crown passed to Anne, the second daughter of James II. Sadly, every one of Queen Anne's 17 children died, so the crown passed to a German prince who was the great-grandson of James I. He became George I in 1714.

The Industrial Revolution

George I's son succeeded him as George II, and was the last reigning monarch ever to lead his troops into battle. The next king, George III, was the grandson of George II. He came to the throne in 1760, and reigned for 59 years until his death in 1820. These years saw the start of the Industrial Revolution in England. People began to move away from the farms and villages into the towns where they could get jobs in the new manufacturing industries such as textiles. It was also during George III's reign that England's colonies in North America objected to the taxes that the English parliament imposed. This led to war, which the Americans won, and the new United States of America had to be recognized as an independent nation.

From 1801 onward George III suffered from bouts of insanity and by 1810 was totally insane. His son acted as Regent from that date, becoming king as George IV on his father's death. He reigned for another ten years. It was during his reign that the first passenger railroad in the world came into being, between Stockton and Darlington in the north of England.

The Victorian age
Next in line was King William IV and then, in 1837, Queen Victoria, who was to be the longest reigning monarch England has ever had. Her reign lasted 64 years. During that time the British Empire reached its peak, with overseas possessions that included New Zealand, Australia, India, Burma, South Africa, and parts of the Pacific. There were advances in many different directions in Victoria's reign. Charles Darwin published his famous work on evolution, *The Origin of Species*. Joseph Lister introduced the antiseptic system to modern surgery, and

During the reign of Queen Victoria, the Industrial Revolution was at its peak. In 1851, the Great Exhibition was opened by Victoria to demonstrate to the world the industrial abilities of England, and to show the English nation aspects of life in England's many colonies. The exhibition was held in the Crystal Palace which was specially built out of glass and iron. The exhibition contained 13,000 exhibits.

Florence Nightingale reformed nursing by introducing hygiene into British Army hospitals. The Penny Post, the first mail to use stamps, was started, and the London subway was begun.

When Queen Victoria died in 1901, in the first year of the twentieth century, England along with the rest of the world was beginning to wake up to new ideas of all kinds. Two years after Victoria's eldest son came to the throne as Edward VII, the suffragette movement was started, to get women the right to vote for parliament. (Women got full voting rights in 1928.) Later in his reign, old age pensions were introduced. Edward VII was a popular king and made many visits abroad to help international relations. When he died in 1910 his funeral was attended by no fewer than nine European kings and seven queens.

World War I

Edward's brother, George V, was the next king. In 1914 Great Britain declared war on Germany. This was World War I, between the Allied Powers (Britain, France, Russia, Italy, and the United States) and the Central Powers (Germany, Austria-Hungary, and Turkey). Many lives were lost before it finally ended with Germany's defeat, in 1918. At this time, George V took the name Windsor, for political reasons.

The first radio broadcasts by the BBC (British Broadcasting Corporation) came along in the early 1920s and the jet engine was invented by Frank Whittle. A depression started in 1929 that was to last several years in England, bringing mass unemployment and unhappiness.

In 1931 the Commonwealth of Nations was formed, which marked the full independence of many of Britain's former colonies and the end of the great age of the British Empire.

When George V died in 1936, his eldest son took the throne as Edward VIII. He wanted, however, to marry Mrs. Wallis Simpson, an American who had been divorced. Both the Church and the state were opposed. Rather than give up the marriage, Edward VIII abdicated, leaving the throne to his brother, George VI.

A changing nation

Three years later, in 1939, the country was at war with Germany again, in World War II. Again millions of people died, including civilians.

On his 40th birthday Prince Charles, heir to the throne of England, attended a party in his honor. This party was organized by the many people that have benefited from his projects for helping young people in deprived areas. In recent years the image of the monarchy has changed. They spend more time now helping others.

George VI's reign lasted until 1952, when his elder daughter became queen as Elizabeth II. Her reign has seen considerable changes. Women have become a force in the country, and the first English woman prime minister, Margaret Thatcher, came to power in 1979. Technology has taken an enormous leap forward in such areas as nuclear power and laser and optical fiber technology. Interest is being taken in conservation of all kinds, from endangered animals and plants to historic buildings.

3   Life in England

England is very densely populated. This small country has only one thousandth of all the land in the world, but over 47 million people live there. That is one eightieth of the world's population! For every square mile in England, there are 915 people. Out of every 25 of those people, at least one is in England as an immigrant from either Pakistan or another country of the New Commonwealth such as Malaysia or Singapore. These people left their home countries in the hope of getting work and having a better standard of living in England.

All over England the language spoken is English, but the way it is spoken in Yorkshire in the

London has many tourists who come to see its shops, museums, and historical buildings. At Christmas time one of its well-known attractions are the lights that decorate the main shopping areas around Oxford Street and Regent Street.

north can sound quite different from the way it is spoken in Cornwall in the south, for example. However, everyone can understand one another.

The Green Capital

Over three-quarters of the people in England live in towns and cities. About seven million people live in the capital city, London. It is known as the green capital because it has so many large parks and open spaces. The Thames River which flows through London has itself become a major tourist attraction. At 210 miles long, the Thames is the longest river in England, and the most important.

Another interesting part of London is the City, where many of England's banks and money exchanges have their offices. It is said to be the richest place in the world. London also has many neighborhoods, such as Tower Hamlets, which are extremely poor.

There are many cafes and restaurants in London, but people who work in London often take a lunch from home with them. In summer-time, park benches everywhere are full of people eating sandwiches and enjoying the sunshine.

The government

England is governed from London, by the Houses of Parliament where all the laws are made. The Houses of Parliament are split into two parts. Members of the House of Lords, known as the upper house, are peers and peeresses who do not have to be elected. They either inherit their membership or are asked to become a member. The men and women who are members of the

This is a painting of the interior of the House of Commons because photographs cannot be taken. The members of the House are seated on both sides with the Government on the left and the Opposition on the right. The members on the Front Benches are the most powerful on each side, and include the leaders of the parties. In the galleries above are members of the public who have come to hear the proceedings.

House of Commons, however, have been elected by the people of England to represent them.

The main political parties in England are the Conservative Party, the Labour Party, the Social Democratic and Liberal Party, and the Social Democrats. At the moment, there are more Conservative members in the House of Commons than members of any other party. They have the majority, and the party in the House of Commons with a majority is known as the government, with the power to run England as it thinks best.

The party with the next largest number of members is the Opposition Party, which at the moment is Labour. The Opposition Party tests all the decisions the government makes by asking questions in the House of Commons which the government must answer. This system of electing representatives and questioning their actions is one form of democracy.

Industrial cities

After London, Birmingham is England's next largest city. Unlike the capital, however, it does not have a large number of parks, and factories and houses exist side by side. As many as 1,500 different kinds of industries can be found in Birmingham: more than anywhere else in England. For instance, the city is a major producer of hardware goods, cars, plastics, buttons, medals, tires, and chocolate. The other largest cities are farther north. Their large populations were a result of the expansion of industry in the nineteenth century. Manchester has expanded from its industrial origins and has become an important center for commerce and banking. Leeds and Bradford grew to importance as the result of a flourishing textile trade. Although textiles still play a part, both cities have a wide variety of industries, and Bradford has developed a thriving tourist trade as a center for the history of the Industrial Revolution. Sheffield is the center of the special steel and cutlery industries, and Liverpool was one of the greatest trading centers of the world. Most of these cities were badly affected by severe unemployment during the early 1980s and some of the traditional industries have died out. However, the magnificence of many of their municipal buildings, both old and new, are a reminder of their heritage.

Home life

Family life in England has been changing over the years. Mothers used to stay at home to look after children, clean the house, and cook meals, while fathers went out to work to earn money. Today, however, many mothers go out to work, and cooking, cleaning, and looking after their children is often shared by both parents. If mother and father both go to work, young children may be looked after by a nanny or a baby sitter.

This is the city center of Sheffield, showing both older and brand new buildings. Bomb damage during World War II and razing of slum houses have allowed town planners to build dramatic new developments.

Unemployment has also brought about a change in many families. If the father is unemployed and the mother has a job, it is often the father who will do the cooking and housework while the mother earns the money. In a one-parent family there is only one parent, either the mother or the father, to do all the work.

Whatever kind of family it may be, the size of a typical family is decreasing. There are fewer children in each household today than there were 20 years ago. In addition, families are getting smaller because elderly people now live in their own homes or in group homes especially built for them, rather than with their adult children.

Religion

The official religion in England is Christianity and Queen Elizabeth II, as reigning monarch, is head of the Church of England. Only about one person in every eight in England is a practicing Christian, however. There are today many other religions practiced in England, such as Hinduism, Islam, Judaism, and Sikhism. Some people have no religion at all. Nevertheless, although there are so many different religious faiths in the country, the English year is marked by Christian holidays.

The most popular Christian festival is Christmas Day, on December 25, which celebrates the birth of Jesus Christ. More people go to church on this day than at any other time of the year, many of them attending midnight carol services.

There are other customs in England associated with Christmas which are nonreligious, including, for example, decorating a Christmas tree with brightly colored glass balls and tinsel. Children also hang stockings and pillowcases on the ends of their beds on Christmas Eve, hoping that Father Christmas will bring them presents.

Shrove Tuesday

Another Christian date in the English year is Shrove Tuesday. This marks the start of the 40 days of Lent. Traditionally Lent was a time when people gave up eating meat, so every last scrap of animal fat had to be used up before the period of Lent started. For this purpose pancakes were made, and Shrove Tuesday quickly became known as Pancake Day. The art of "tossing the pancake" soon developed into something of a sport, and on Pancake Day each year races are held throughout England. One of the most famous races is held in London. Housewives, chefs, TV personalities, and beauty queens gather together to run a 100-yard course, tossing their pancakes as they go. It's a popular event, and large crowds cheer them on.

After Lent comes Easter, again a Christian festival. Easter for children is marked by the giving and receiving of chocolate Easter eggs. Both Christmas and Easter are holidays for people in England, whatever their religion.

Other special festivals
People of the Jewish faith living in England have their own festivals. At their new year festival of Rosh Hashanah, many of the foods eaten are made with honey in the hope that the new year will be kind and sweet. Hindu people have this custom as well, making sure that at least one sweet dish is eaten on the first day of the new year, which is said to be a day of new beginnings.

For Muslims, the new year and other festivals have different dates each year. This is because Muslims follow the Islamic faith and the Islamic year is shorter than a calendar year. An important part of Muslim life is fasting, when a Muslim must not eat or drink between daybreak and sunset.

They do this during their month of Ramadan; at the end of Ramadan there is a huge feast.

Bonfire Night

Many customs in England are not religious festivals. One of the most popular customs is having a bonfire on Guy Fawkes night. Bonfire Night, as it is also called, is always November 5, to mark the occasion when Guy Fawkes and his friends tried to blow up the Houses of Parliament in the seventeenth century. Until recently it was celebrated by individual families each having their own bonfire in their gardens and setting off a few fireworks. However, so many children have been badly burned in the past that now community Bonfire Night events are often organized by a town or village. At these events, really big bonfires are lit and there are exciting fireworks.

May Day

The first day of May, known as May Day, is also celebrated in many parts of England, sometimes by dancing around a Maypole. Long, brightly colored ribbons are attached to the top of a high pole, then a number of dancers each holding a ribbon weave around the pole to lively tunes. There may also be some Morris Men present, dressed in white shirts and trousers, with bells on their legs. They dance traditional dances in time to the music from an accordion.

At Halloween it is children who dress up, this time as witches. Halloween is always October 31, and it is said to be the night of the witches. Children play special games, like bobbing for apples and making pumpkin lanterns.

4 The Changing Farm

In the nineteenth century, farming was only just beginning to be helped by machinery. In this dairy of the 1860s, the dairymaid is able to make butter by turning the handle on the butter churn. In the righthand corner is an old-fashioned churn where the long wooden pole had to be moved up and down and around, which was much harder work. The cheeses in the background are being held in a metal cheese press.

England was a farming country until the end of the eighteenth century. Most people earned their living from the land. They either worked on large farms or looked after their own small farms producing enough food to support their families. Any extra produce was bought and sold at the nearest market. People lived in tight-knit village communities and few traveled very far from their homes.

The move to towns

In the 1800s this rural way of life was completely altered by the Industrial Revolution. Transportation systems improved, with first the canals and then the railroads to carry goods and raw materials from one part of the country to another.

There were many new inventions for weaving cloth and forging iron and steel. Lastly, factories and mills were located near coalfields where there was a ready source of power.

For some time, fewer workers had been needed to produce food because of earlier changes in agricultural methods, so now people began to move away from the land to find jobs in industrial areas. Many villages expanded into towns and cities. Today only a very small proportion of the working population (2.5 percent) is employed on the land. There are still villages but over three-quarters of England's 47 million people live in towns and cities. Many village shops and schools have closed and people now must travel to the nearest town for groceries, entertainment, or even for education.

England is no longer dependent on agriculture for wealth and employment. Nevertheless, agriculture is still a very important industry, because about 62 percent of the food needed by the population is produced within England. Although the climate is too cold for some foods such as bananas, tea, and coffee, England is self-sufficient in eggs, milk, and wheat. Farmland occupies a lot of space in England, yet there are not many farms. This is because the trend now is away from the old-style small family-run farms to much larger high-production units where machines do most of the work. The result is that there are fewer farms and farm workers but the size and efficiency of farms has increased and productivity is very high. The average size of a farm in England is now around 124 acres, five times larger than 40 years ago.

Types of farming

The geography, soil, and climate of England are so varied that no two farms are alike. Farmers have to adapt to the conditions. The main types of farming nowadays are arable (crop growing), livestock (animals), and horticulture (fruit and vegetables). Traditionally farms had both livestock and crops but today the majority of farmers specialize in one type of farming. Most of the arable farms are in the east and south of the country where the land is flat and the climate is milder and drier. One of the most common crops grown in England is wheat which is used to make flour and breakfast cereals. Other crops are barley, used as malt to make beer and whisky, and rapeseed, used in cooking oil, margarine, and paint. Potatoes and sugar beet are also grown. More farmers in the east of the country and the West Midlands are now growing fruit such as strawberries and apples, and vegetables such as cabbages, onions, and Brussels sprouts. Growing vegetables on farms is known as market gardening. Often customers come to these farms to pick their own produce for a lower price.

Dairy farming

Cattle are either reared and fattened for beef or kept as dairy cows for their milk. Dairy cattle are usually kept in the west of England where there is plenty of rain and the grass is rich. The most common dairy cow is the Friesian which is black and white. Milk is one of the most important products on farms in England. The average person drinks about three pints of milk a week. A typical dairy cow will produce around 1,078 gallons of

Today many farms are highly mechanized. This farm uses the latest technology on a rotary milking parlor. Several cows can be milked at the same time and the dairyman is able to see clearly everything that is going on. He is also helped by electronic monitoring machinery.

milk a year, that's 8,624 pint cartons. The milk is pasteurized and bottled on the farm or in nearby dairies and then either delivered directly to the doorstep or to shops and supermarkets. Milk is also used for dairy products such as butter and cheese. Sheep are kept for their meat, as lamb or mutton, and also for their wool.

Mechanized farming

One of the greatest changes in the last 40 years is that most farm jobs can now be done by machines. There are no longer any working horses, and machinery is highly sophisticated and complex. Computers are often used to plan feeding programs and work out the daily running

Huge combine harvesters are used in many places to harvest grain quickly. Both the combines and the tractors are very big, so on a lot of farms the fields have been made larger by pulling out the hedgerows.

of the farm. Large tractors pull plows, cultivators, sprayers, and other machines. Grain is harvested by a complex combine harvester and most dairy farms have an automated milking parlor instead of milking cows by hand. The machines used are powerful and efficient so, although the operators must be trained and skilled, fewer people are needed. Work can often be given to outside contractors so that the farmer does not need to own big machines that may stand idle much of the year.

New techniques

New farming techniques have also increased the output. Farmers now grow improved crop varieties that give a higher yield and new ideas on breeding and feeding animals mean they can produce more milk and meat. Most farmers today also use artificial fertilizers to enrich their land and pesticides and herbicides to fight diseases, pests, and weeds. Over the past few years, however, many people have objected to the use of these chemicals and a small number of farmers grow their produce without chemical fertilizers or pesticides. This is called organic farming and their produce is available throughout the country.

There's been a change in the actual look of the farms and the countryside, too. Buildings made of prefabricated material are now more common than the old farm buildings and barns that were centered on the farmyard where chickens used to strut around. Until after World War II fields were small, with hedges and trees acting as fences and providing shelter. The different fields looked rather like a patchwork quilt. Since then many ponds, once a feature of farms, have been filled in and a large number of hedgerows have now been removed so that larger and more economical fields can be organized.

Hedgerows

Hedgerows have always provided a natural habitat for wild flowers, butterflies, birds such as blackbirds and sparrows and small mammals like hedgehogs. Destroying the hedgerows to create larger fields has endangered the survival of several species of wildlife. It has also allowed the top soil to blow away, even creating dust storms in places such as East Anglia. Over the past few years some farmers and conservationists have been working to replace what has been lost by reinstalling hedgerows, although the landscape will never look quite the same again. In some places new trees and hedges have been planted and new ponds have been created. There are also experts who will advise farmers on how to conserve wildlife on their land without reinstalling the hedgerows.

Intensive farming

Sheep and cattle are a familiar sight grazing on the hilly and moorland areas of northern and southwestern England. Pigs and poultry, however, are by far the most numerous animals on a farm. In fact, in Great Britain as a whole there are more than 128 million egg-laying hens, turkeys, and broilers (chickens bred for meat); that is, more than twice the number of people living there. The reason pigs and poultry are not very visible is that they are usually housed in intensive units. These units are especially built so that the environment can be carefully controlled and no disease can enter. One unit may contain thousands of chickens, so crowded together that they cannot get any exercise. Intensive farming is economic and convenient, bringing production up and costs down. Each hen in an intensive unit produces around 220 eggs a year. However, many people worry about the welfare of animals living in such unnatural conditions, without sunlight or fresh air. The Farm Animals Welfare Council has

Although many jobs on farms have been mechanized some still have to be done by hand. Fruit picking requires a lot of labor so many fruit farmers prefer to sell the fruit slightly cheaper and allow people to pick their own.

drawn up a code of practice to ensure all stock living in these conditions are cared for properly. There is also concern over how to get rid of the waste from animals in intensive units. Unless the "slurry," as the liquid manure is called, is disposed of carefully it can pollute the waterways and destroy fish.

Common agricultural policy

The highly scientific and mechanized farming techniques of the past 40 years have brought great leaps in productivity. In the 1980s a cow produces twice as much milk and a field of wheat more than double the amount of grain than once was the case. In fact, the country is producing more than the population needs. At a time when there are such shortages of food in the Third World, the extra food has led to much debate. England is a member of the European Community (EC) which sets a Common Agricultural Policy (CAP) for its members. CAP protects farmers by ensuring a set price for goods. If the market price falls below the agreed limit, then the EC buys the produce from the farmers and keeps it in storage until the demand is higher and a better price can be gained. However, productivity is now so high that the food is forming stored "mountains" of cereals and "lakes" of milk that are no good to anyone. England and other countries in the EC are discussing ways of stopping this waste without reducing the farmers' income. One proposal is alternative use of land. Farmers are being encouraged to use their land for other things than growing crops or keeping livestock. Ideas include building sports facilities, setting up farm shops and pick-your-own centers, opening nature trails and exhibitions, or turning farms into resorts. Fish farming is also expanding, with salmon, trout, and shellfish being bred for food or oil.

5　Industry and Trade

England is one of the richest countries in the world. It is a highly industrialized society, with three main types of industries providing both wealth and employment. They are known as the primary industries, the secondary or manufacturing industries, and the tertiary or service industries.

The primary industries produce raw materials and food. These include agriculture, forestry, fishing, and mining and quarrying for coal, oil, gas, and minerals. Around three percent of the working population is employed in the primary industries.

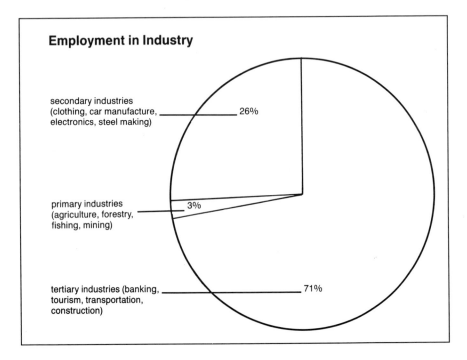

Employment in Industry

secondary industries (clothing, car manufacture, electronics, steel making)　26%

primary industries (agriculture, forestry, fishing, mining)　3%

tertiary industries (banking, tourism, transportation, construction)　71%

The secondary or manufacturing industries process the products of primary industries, from England and other countries, to make goods. Strawberries are made into jam, for example, and china clay into cups and saucers. These industries provide jobs for just over 26 percent of the workforce.

Tertiary or service industries include banking, tourism, transportation and construction, among others. Until the 1970s, if you asked a class of children what their fathers did for a living, most of them would have said that he had a job in one of the primary or secondary industries. Today most children would answer that he worked in one of the service industries, since these now provide employment for over 70 percent of the working people in England.

Nationalized industries

Some industries such as British Coal, British Rail, the Post Office, and the electricity supply industry are nationalized: that is, they are owned and run by the state. The government policy during the 1980s has been to sell these industries to private firms to create both more efficiency and greater competition. The government also encourages people to set up their own businesses and there are now many small businesses making a variety of goods and providing services of all kinds.

When the Industrial Revolution first turned England into an industrial power, the country built its wealth on its manufacturing industries, especially iron and steel and textiles. Until the 1950s English shipbuilders built around a third of the world's ships, and boilers, engines, bridges, and other kinds of heavy machinery were made in England.

Each industry has its own special needs, and these industries grew up in different locations. The woolen industry, for example, was based in Lancashire where sheep provided the wool, and coal from the nearby coalfields could be used to fuel the steam-powered machinery. The steel industry grew up in the Midlands and north near both iron ore deposits and coalfields.

Energy supply

The most important need for any industry is a supply of energy, that is, fuel of some kind to run the machines. England has always had more than enough for its needs. Coal was traditionally the most important source of energy and still provides over a third of the amount needed. The coal industry has declined since the 1920s as other fuels have taken its place, and many coal mines have been closed. New mechanized mines are now being opened, however, such as Selby coalfield in Yorkshire. But fewer workers are needed, which is not helping those unemployed.

The recent discovery of reserves of oil and natural gas in the North Sea means that England is now self-sufficient in oil and gas. The first oil was brought ashore in 1975, and by 1980 there was enough for the country's own needs and for export, too. However, the reserves may run out within the next ten years and so surveys to find new oilfields both on land and under the sea are being carried out.

England has large resources of oil in the North Sea. These "roughnecks" are attending to the drill that goes down through the oil rig into the sea bed. The work demands speed and strength, as adding new lengths of pipe or changing the drilling bit has to be done as quickly as possible. Workers on oil rigs are well paid for dangerous work.

New types of energy

In 1956, England established the world's first large-scale nuclear power station, at Calder Hall in Cumbria, and nuclear power now provides much of England's long-term energy. However, many people are worried about the dangers of nuclear power, and the problem of what to do with the radioactive waste. Research is now being carried out to find different sources of long-term energy, using wind and water power or solar energy from the sun.

The traditional industries that grew up near sources of energy such as the coalfields are no longer as important as they were. This is partly due to competition from overseas, especially in the heavy engineering industries. Japan is now the world leader in engineering. The decline of these manufacturing industries has led to a great deal of unemployment in the towns and cities that grew up around them, and many people in the northeast and northwest of England have now lost their jobs.

Modern industries

New manufacturing industries are taking the place of the old ones. These are mainly light industries making products such as food, drinks, clothes, and calculators, rather than heavy machinery.

Chemicals, electrical and electronic engineering, vehicle manufacture, textiles, and food processing are the most important industries today. These do not need to be near either a particular source of power or the raw materials they require. The factories, based mainly in the Midlands, London, and the south of England, are highly mechanized. Machines and sophisticated equipment now do much of the work once done by men and women. Robots are often used on the production line in car factories.

The electronics industry is also very important in England nowadays. Many familiar household machines such as washing machines, televisions, stoves, and computers are made in England. The chemical industry is another major source of wealth and employment; its products include

Although heavy industries such as steel-making and ship-building are traditionally found in the north of England, light industries such as vehicle-making are found all over the country. This factory is near Slough, Bucks. Certain parts of this manufacturing process are carried out entirely by robots.

many of the pharmaceutical drugs prescribed by doctors. The chemical industry also produces cosmetics, soaps, dyes, plastics, paints, and the artificial fibers such as nylon, polyester, and acrylics used in many clothes today.

Over a million people are employed making vehicles, and leading car manufacturers in England are Austin Rover, Ford, and Vauxhall. Two world famous specialist car firms are Rolls-Royce and Jaguar. Rolls-Royce cars are renowned

Although this appears to be a sleepy little place it is part of one of England's main industries — tourism. This is the small town of Dunster in north Somerset. Although it only has a population of about 1,000, thousands of tourists visit the town each year to see its ancient castle and the yarn market in the picturesque village street.

for comfort and quality, and the majority of the cars built since 1904 can still be driven on the roads. A large number of people also work in aerospace factories making parts for aircraft, jet engines, military and space equipment.

The service industries have grown rapidly over the past few years. Tourism is one of the main service industries, employing over a million people. That number is increasing year by year as more and more people take vacations in England. London is a leading tourist center, with popular attractions such as the Tower of London and Madame Tussaud's wax museum. All over England people have jobs in museums, art galleries, historic houses and castles, resort areas, theme parks, hotels, and restaurants.

All over the country there are museums. Some of these are "living" museums, such as the Acton Scott Working Farm Museum in Shropshire. These people are working on the farm in the way it was done before the invention of the tractor. They are dressed in the clothes of an earlier age and are using the traditional Shropshire wagon. Visitors are able to see how much life on a farm has changed.

The European Community

England as part of the United Kingdom is one of the world's leading trading nations, exporting around 30 percent of English goods and services to other countries. The discovery of North Sea oil has had a great impact on the pattern of trade, since oil no longer has to be imported and there is enough surplus to export. Joining the European Community (EC) in 1973 meant a change in the United Kingdom's main trading partners. Until then most trade was with North America and the Commonwealth countries; now trade with members of the EC, especially West Germany, Netherlands, and France has greatly increased. The aim of the EC is to organize a community where people and goods can move freely without any barriers or restrictions. Already the member countries follow common policies in agriculture and trade and 1992 is the year set for the EC to be one single market.

6   Keeping in Touch

Over a million people travel into London to go to work each day. Many more travel to other cities, towns, and villages at home and overseas either for work or pleasure. Thousands of tons of goods must be transported between England and destinations all over the world. All this is made possible by a network of road, rail, sea, and air transportation systems.

Roads are the most important means of travel throughout England and Great Britain. About 81 percent of all goods are carried by trucks and 90 percent of all passengers travel by road. Roads vary in size and capacity. The smallest roads are the country lanes used mainly by farm vehicles and local people but there are also much busier roads that often have dual sets of lanes and carry a great deal of traffic. The busiest roads are super-highways that provide essential links between the main cities and industrial areas. Although they make up only one percent of the total length of roads, the 39 superhighways in England carry around 15 percent of the traffic. They are designed for fast travel and have no traffic circles or traffic lights. The latest highway system to be built is the multilaned beltway system around London, the M25. It is the longest orbital highway in the world.

Traffic problems
There are around 20 million vehicles on the roads in England and as many as three-quarters of these are privately owned cars, mopeds, and

The highways in England are very busy. During rush hours when people are traveling to and from work they often become so crowded that the traffic comes to a halt. This highway is the M25 which carries traffic around the outskirts of London. It is so busy that, although it has only recently been built, it is already being widened. (In England, people drive on the left, and cars have the driver's wheels on the right.)

motorcycles. Despite the rising cost of oil the number of people owning cars is increasing and now about three out of every five people have the use of at least one car. All drivers must pass a driving test before they are allowed to drive alone on the road. The minimum age for driving cars and motorbikes is 17 years and for mopeds, 16 years. A speed limit is set at 70 mph on highways and superhighways and 30 mph in built-up areas. The main attraction of cars is the freedom they allow. However, they cause problems, too. There are many accidents on the road. In recent years action has been taken to stop people drinking alcohol and then driving. The building of roads has also destroyed some of England's countryside and natural habitats for wildflowers and animals. Traffic congestion is already a problem both on highways and in the major towns in England and it is likely to get worse because road traffic is expected to rise by at least 40 percent by the end of the century. Some people go by bicycle because of traffic jams and parking difficulties. Cycle lanes are now in use in a number of towns. Many people use public transportation. Another way to get about is to hire a minicab or taxi. It can be expensive but it means you can travel from door to door in the shortest possible time. Black, roomy taxi cabs are a familiar sight in London streets.

In the large cities like London, buses and taxis are a very popular form of transportation. The traffic is very crowded in the narrow streets and it is difficult to find a parking space, so many people avoid bringing their own cars into the city.

When the first passenger line was opened in 1815 people were often afraid to travel on the trains as they felt they went too fast at 15 mph! The carriages they traveled in were just coach bodies fixed onto wheels designed to roll on tracks. During the next 60 years nearly 17,000 miles of track were laid to make a network over the whole country.

Public transportation

The cheapest form of public transportation is by bus. Bus services operate in local areas taking people to the stores, school, or the office. The number of bus services available, however, is getting smaller and smaller as more people rely on the car. Some buses take passengers farther distances, sometimes abroad.

Traveling by rail is more costly than by bus but much faster. Many of the lines have been electrified and high-speed trains can go as fast as 125 mph.

Railroads formed an important part of England's industrial growth and many towns grew up around them. The world's first

These high-speed trains standing at Paddington Station in London show how far rail travel has come in just over 150 years. They are known as 125s as their sleek design allows them to travel at speeds of over 125 mph. They are used on long runs and have cut journey times dramatically. This allows some people to live a very long way from their work.

passenger public rail service was the Stockton and Darlington Railway which was opened in 1825. By the 1960s new forms of transportation meant that railways were proving unprofitable and many lines and stations were closed in 1963. Today few goods are transported by rail, but about seven percent of all passenger travel is on the railway network. Major towns and cities are connected by fast trains and there are also slower locals that stop at most stations on a line. Commuter services mean that workers can live farther from the main cities but travel to and from work each day. Some people now live over 100 miles from their job but still commute daily.

England can boast the first subway in the world. Opened in London in 1863 as a way of avoiding the congestion on the streets, London Underground Railway has expanded and is now one of the largest in the world, carrying more than 14 million passengers every week. It is often known as the "tube." There are also subway systems in Liverpool and in Newcastle upon Tyne.

Water transportation
Inland waterways were important for transporting raw materials and goods in the eighteenth century. England's rivers and canals are now used mainly for pleasure. People enjoy traveling in boats and barges on the inland waterways for day trips and longer vacations. However, a few goods are still carried, and there are plans to open up unused canals.

A high proportion of overseas trade is by sea, and England has a large merchant navy fleet. The main ports are London, Tees and Hartlepool, Grimsby, Felixstowe, Southampton, Liverpool, and Manchester. New machinery has been brought into the ports in recent years to keep up with the new methods of shipping. Goods are now stored in large metal containers so that they can be lifted by crane as one unit. This is easily transferred from a truck to a container ship, where goods are carried above deck as well as below. Another new development is the roll-on roll-off ship which can carry trucks complete with their loads. Air travel is so available now that few passengers go long distances by sea. A third of all travelers between England and the rest of Europe, however, do still go by ferry or hovercraft.

Air travel

England has seven main airports and many smaller regional ones. London's Heathrow Airport is one of the busiest international airports in the world, so busy that a new terminal had to be added recently. Many of England's other airports have been extended and modernized to cope with the rapidly growing demand for air travel both within Great Britain and abroad. The whole world is opening up to travelers as the number of flights and possible destinations increase. Air travel is getting much faster, too. During recent years, airports have become more important for overseas trade, for planes are ideal for carrying small, light, and valuable goods such as scientific instruments and computer software.

Scientists and engineers in England are joining others from all over the world in the search for faster, more efficient ways of sending and receiving information within the country and abroad. Some of the world's first experiments in global satellite communications took place at Goonhilly Downs in Cornwall in the early 1960s. England is now connected by satellite to over 80 countries through telephone and television links. A typical satellite telephone call from a home or office in England goes first to the local exchange, then the international exchange, and then to a huge dish aerial at an Earth station. It is then beamed up to a satellite, over 23,000 miles out in space, from which it is beamed down to an Earth station in another country. The satellite network means people in England can watch television broadcasts of events such as the Olympic Games wherever they are held.

These huge dishes look like alien visitors from outer space! They are part of England's satellite communications network. The dishes take up a lot of land so they are situated well away from big cities. These are in the rural county of Hereford and are receiving telephone signals bouncing off satellites in orbit around the Earth.

Optical fiber network

Communications inside the country have been revolutionized with the use of optical fibers, which are hair-thin strands of pure glass that carry information as pulses of light. The major cities in England are already linked and the optical fiber network will soon be carried abroad by undersea cables. All types of communication can be carried along an optical fiber cable; pictures, music, voice, text, and computer data are a few examples. Optical fibers open up many new opportunities. Already cable television channels are being transmitted into homes and people are beginning to refer to the "wired society" where banking, shopping, and perhaps even schoolwork can be done from home.

These advances have had a huge effect on the way business is conducted. Every office in England has a telephone and you can dial directly to 185 countries; that is 93 percent of the telephones in the world. A telephone paging system means that people can be contacted wherever they are, and an answer machine will record messages while you're out. Many telephones are mobile; some are installed in cars. A few offices can even hold video conferences with people in different parts of the country.

Office computers
Central to every large office is a computer that stores essential data. The more sophisticated computers have links with other computers at home and abroad and can give and receive information. Most offices in England, even small businesses, have at least one computer with word processing facilities. These are electronic typewriters with a display screen and computer memory, and they relieve secretaries of a lot of time-consuming typing work. Written messages between offices in England and other countries can be sent by telex machines or the speedier, more efficient facsimile machines. These "fax" machines can communicate words and pictures to someone else within seconds.

The communications revolution has not really

affected people in their homes yet. Many people have their own personal computers but very few are linked to others. The telephone is the main means of communication in the home. Most households have a telephone and there are many public pay phones in streets and buildings around the country, often with a phone card facility so that coins are no longer needed.

The postal system
Letters and parcels are sent by mail. The postal system has been modernized in recent years and each postal address now has a postal code so letters can be mechanically sorted into areas and streets. Letters sent first class from one town in England usually arrive at another town in England on the next weekday, and have priority over second class which is cheaper. News from home and abroad is communicated through the press and by television and radio broadcasting. Three out of every four adults read at least one newspaper a day. There are about a dozen national daily newspapers and hundreds of regional and local newspapers with news and features of special interest to the area. The oldest, most established newspaper is *The Times* which was first published over 200 years ago.

There are four main television channels. Two channels are run by the BBC and financed by license fees paid by households with a television set. The other two are commercial channels with advertisements. Satellite communications and cable television channels are giving English people a wider choice of television viewing. Radio is another important medium for news.

7 Off to School

When children get to primary school at 5-years old they are not only taught to read, write, and do arithmetic, they are encouraged to paint, draw, sing, and do drama. Many schools have children of different cultures. The teachers help them to learn about each other's different lifestyles.

In England, all children between the age of 5 and 16 must go to school and receive full time education. They may attend a state school, which is free for everyone, or they can go to a private school, for which their parents must pay a fee each term. Most children go to state schools, but about seven percent are sent to private schools. Although the law only requires children over the age of 5 to go to school, as many as 43 percent of parents are now choosing to send their 3- and 4-year olds to nursery schools where they can meet other children and prepare for infant school.

These secondary school children are taught in a more formal way. They work on a wider range of subjects than at primary school, adding geography, history, design and technology, a foreign language, and cooking to their lessons. At the end of each year they have class examinations to check on how well they are learning.

In the state system, infant school is where 5- to 7-year olds are taught to read and write and to do some arithmetic. Infants also spend a great deal of time doing art and music, playing and having fun! Most children pass from infant school to junior school (where they usually learn a wider range of subjects) when they are 7 years old. They go on to secondary school when they are about 11. However, in some parts of England there are "first" schools for pupils aged 5 to around 9 years and "middle" schools for pupils aged between about 8 and 14 years. Most English state-run secondary schools are comprehensive, which means that they will take all the girls and boys from one particular district regardless of their ability. Children go to school every weekday from

9 a.m. to 3:30 p.m. in most cases. At most schools children are required to wear a uniform, and at others they wear their ordinary everyday clothes. The school day starts with registration when each pupil's name is recorded in the register. Some schools also start the day with school assembly which may include hymns and a prayer. Most pupils have their lunch at school. They may eat sandwiches brought from home, or a meal prepared in the school kitchens or brought by a mobile kitchen. The meal can vary from sausages or baked fish served with boiled vegetables or a salad to hamburgers and french fries, followed by dessert such as a sweet tart or just an apple.

Children stay at a comprehensive school until they are 16, the earliest age at which they are allowed to leave school. Some then leave school and try to find work. If their school has higher grades they may stay on for another one or two years before going on to further education at technical and other colleges. Alternatively, they may go on to a "sixth form" college where they study until they are 18. A different form of state-run secondary school is available in a few parts of England, known as a grammar school. (Some grammar schools are independent.) Pupils gain a place at a grammar school by passing an examination, usually at the age of 11. Those children who fail the examination are sent to "secondary modern" schools. Some children who have special educational needs, who may, for instance, have learning difficulties or some form of physical or mental handicap, are unable to attend an ordinary school. These children learn at special schools.

Children who have learning difficulties, as a result of a physical problem such as blindness or damaged limbs, are often taught in special schools. However, whenever possible, they are encouraged to work with other children, so that the children can learn from each other.

Private schools

Children whose parents pay fees for their education attend private schools known as independent schools or public schools. These range from small nurseries to large boarding schools and include some schools for children from particular ethnic minorities or of specific religions. Children go to private school either daily or as boarders, living in the school and only going home on weekends or for holidays. After nursery school, children attending private schools usually go to preparatory school, so-called because it prepares children for the Common Entrance Examination which they need to pass in order to enter senior school. Pupils attend senior school from the age of about 11 until they are 18 or 19.

Very similar subjects are taught at all schools; including mathematics, English, science, foreign languages, history, geography, music, art, sports and, increasingly, computer science. Around the age of 16 pupils take examinations to gain their General Certificate of Secondary Education, known as the GCSE. Children who attend school after the age of 16 often take GCE A (A stands for advanced) level examinations in two or three of their best subjects. GCE A levels or their equivalent must be passed by all pupils hoping to go on to study at a university, a polytechnic school, or a college of higher education.

Further education

Over one-third of England's young people receive some form of education after leaving school. Young people who go to a polytechnic school or a university usually study for three or four years full time, depending on the course chosen. At the end of their period of study they take examinations. Students who pass their examinations are awarded what is known as a degree. The two most common first degrees awarded are Bachelor of Arts, known as a BA, and Bachelor of Science, known as a BSc. If students continue to study they may be awarded a Master of Arts degree known as an MA, or a Master of Science degree known as an MSc. Finally, a Doctor of Philosophy degree, a PhD, may be awarded, usually for research. The best-known universities in England are Oxford and Cambridge. They were started in the twelfth and thirteenth centuries. All the other universities in England were founded in the nineteenth and twentieth centuries.

When students at a university have successfully finished their courses they are awarded their degrees at a special ceremony. While they are still studying the students are called undergraduates but when they have their degrees they are known as graduates. These young men and women are new graduates of Cambridge University. To show this they are wearing black gowns trimmed with fur.

Youth Training Schemes

Young people who leave school at 16 and who do not manage to find a job are quite often offered a place on a Youth Training Scheme, known as YTS. It is a government program that tries to give planned work experience to all young people between the ages of 16 and 18. Teenagers placed on a YTS may go into banks, hotels, shops, and factories, or get work experience in hairdressing, tourism, building, catering, engineering, or manufacturing. Each young person on a Youth Training Scheme is given an allowance which is more than an unemployed person receives, but less than an adult person doing the same job would get. For some young people YTS has proved to be a good way to learn about working alongside adults and a good chance to get useful work experience. However, other young people feel that it is wrong that the wage they are given as a trainee in the YTS is below the wage earned by an adult doing the same job. One difficulty about the program is that the standards of training and work experience vary from one place to another.

Apart from school, work, and Youth Training Schemes, English youths take part in a wide range of activities. Among the most popular organizations run for young people are the Scouts and the Girl Guides, which have a combined membership of around one million. The Duke of Edinburgh's Award Scheme is also popular with young people of all ages. Young people who take part are given awards in four areas of challenging activity: helping in the community, expeditions, the development of personal interests and practical skills, and sports achievement.

8   Health and Welfare

Children born in England today can expect to live much longer than their grandparents. The life expectancy for boys born in the 1980s is 71 years and for girls six years more. These figures are very different from the turn of the century when men could only expect to live to 48, and women to 52 years. Improved standards of living, better working conditions, lower birth rate, healthier diet, and the tremendous advances in medical science and facilities all mean people are living longer and longer. Cures have been discovered for some serious illnesses and the technology and skill is available to carry out life-saving operations. Today children are vaccinated against diseases such as tuberculosis that once took many lives. In the 1980s more people are dying from heart attacks, strokes, and cancer.

Standards of housing and hygiene are generally high. Most people live in a private house or apartment. Nearly all houses have baths and inside toilets and over half have central heating.

Many people in England try to look after their health, follow a balanced diet, and take regular exercise. A lot of people have now given up smoking for health reasons although more alcohol is being drunk. The abuse of alcohol and drugs especially by young people is a matter of great concern. Health education is now taught in schools and publicity campaigns promote healthy habits. Advertisements on television warn people of the harmful effects of smoking and taking drugs, and how to avoid AIDS.

At this baby clinic some mothers are discussing their problems with health visitors. The health service provides midwives to help deliver babies, and health visitors, who are trained nurses, to visit the mothers and check on the babies' well-being during the first year. They run clinics where mothers can meet each other and have their children's hearing and development checked.

The social services

Although the standard of living is high in general, not everyone is so fortunate because of the rise in unemployment. Some families have very little money and live in poor housing. There are also thousands of homeless people. The health and welfare of the nation is, by law, the responsibility of central and local governments. Nearly every working person pays taxes that contribute to the running of health and welfare services. The social services are made up of three areas each giving a different kind of help. First, the National Health Service provides medical care for everyone. Second, the personal social services give practical and emotional help to anyone with special needs such as the elderly, children from broken homes, and physically and mentally disabled people. Third, there's the Social Security system of benefits, giving financial help when it is needed to maintain a basic standard of living.

Much of the health care provided by the National Health Service is free to everyone. Drugs prescribed by a doctor, glasses, dental treatment and dentures are all charged for, but no one pays for any of the other services. The National Health Service aims to provide all the health care needed to help make sick people better and to stop healthy people from becoming ill. Everyone, whether old or young, rich or poor, is entitled to the services of doctors, home visits from the district nurse and health visitor, operations and stays in the hospital, emergency treatment for accidents, and any other medical care that they need. In England there is one doctor for every 800 people. In a Third World country such as India there is only one doctor for every 4,000 patients.

There is a great deal of criticism of the National Health Service in England. There are not enough hospital beds to go around and the waiting lists to get into a hospital are very long, sometimes as much as four years. Some people are not prepared to wait for treatment and would sooner pay a doctor or hospital to have it done privately. As many as one in ten people now take out private medical insurance so that they are covered by insurance should they require medical treatment privately. The actual health care is no different, but private doctors and hospitals can provide a much quicker service.

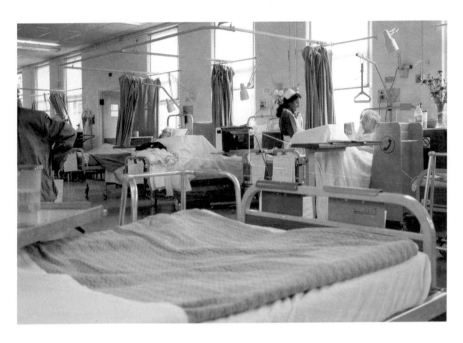

This is an orthopedic ward in a large London hospital. An orthopedic ward treats disorders of the spine, bones, and joints. Most of the people in these wards are elderly as they are more likely to have problems. England, in common with many other countries, has more and more old people in the population. However, as they are less healthy than younger people, this puts strains on the health service.

Alternative medicine

Over recent years there has been a move toward using what is often called "alternative" medicine to help people get well. This is because it is seen as an alternative to usual medical practices. The three main types of treatments are homeopathy, osteopathy, and acupuncture. With homeopathic medicine a person with a disease is given minute amounts of natural drugs that in a healthy person would actually produce symptoms of the illness. An osteopath works by manipulating the bones of the body, and an acupuncturist applies pressure to key points in the body by putting needles through the skin. These treatments may sound strange but trained practitioners know what they are doing. Alternative medicine is growing in popularity. The treatments are usually not available under the National Health Service.

Social workers are employed by local authorities and voluntary organizations to look after the social well-being of the nation. They are qualified to work with the elderly, the mentally and physically handicapped, and children and families with social problems. They give help and advice and make regular visits to homes to check that everything is all right. It is the social worker who watches for signs that children are being cruelly treated by their parents, for example, and must then help to decide whether a child should be taken away from home. They are on call 24 hours a day in case of an emergency.

Volunteer workers
The work of the social workers is backed up by helpers from voluntary organizations such as the Salvation Army, the Women's Royal Voluntary Service, the British Red Cross Society, and St. John Ambulance. Young people also help through community organizations such as Task Force, Community Service Volunteers, Scouts, and Girl Guides. Volunteers may bring "meals on wheels" to housebound people or do their shopping. They run playgroups, drive disabled and elderly people to day centers, assist in hospitals and clinics, and do gardening, or home repairs. Sometimes volunteers simply talk to people who can't get out and meet others.

Many self-help groups have also been set up, run by and for people with certain medical, social, or family problems. They provide up-to-date information as well as practical help and advice on a specific problem. Everyone in the group has the same problem and can get together to offer sympathetic support. Some examples of self-help groups are those for families coping with the death of a loved one, parents with a child who is handicapped or has a diet problem, and people who have suffered from strokes.

Financial help

Social Security provides financial help when it is needed, and there are a variety of benefits. They include benefits for people who are unemployed or retired from work, parents bringing up children, anyone who is sick or disabled, people working on a very low income, and others who do not have enough money to live on. Some people are paid in cash such as retirement pensions, unemployment benefits, and maternity benefits, others come as goods or services. Funds for Social Security benefits come partly from taxation but mainly from National Insurance contributions. Most working people between 16 and pension age (60 for women and 65 for men) have to pay contributions into the National Insurance program. Some benefits are only available to people who have paid into the program, some are given to everyone who needs them. There are many people who don't claim all the benefits that are rightfully theirs, because the system is quite complicated and it is often hard to find out what is available or how to claim it.

9   Having Fun

Cricket is played both as a professional game and as an amateur game. Most towns have their own cricket club and even small villages, such as Lyndhurst in the New Forest, have a team and a village cricket field. Both men and women play cricket and England has had both male and female cricket team world champions.

Most people in England have a surprising amount of spare time. The average working week is now between 35 and 40 hours, which is usually spread over five days. Nearly all workers get at least four weeks' paid vacation a year; some have five weeks. Many households also have time-saving gadgets such as washing machines, food processors, and vacuum cleaners. This gives people time to enjoy hobbies and other interests.

Sports are very popular. There are sports arenas, swimming pools, playing fields, golf

Although outdoor sports are popular, England's rainy climate has encouraged a great interest in indoor activities! Most towns have at least one gymnasium where swimming, judo, and games, such as badminton, squash, or indoor bowling, can be played. This sports center also offers facilities for table tennis, trampolining, and even has a false rock face to practice rock climbing!

courses, tennis courts, skating rinks, gymnasiums, lakes, and parks where people of all ages and abilities can try different sports. It's estimated that about a third of all adults actually take part in a sporting activity at least once a month but many more watch it either live or on television. Most schools provide indoor and outdoor facilities for their pupils to play both competitive and noncompetitive sports.

Among the most famous spectator events on the English sporting calendar are the Lawn Tennis Championships at Wimbledon, the rowing races at Henley Regatta in Oxfordshire, and the Grand National, the world's best-known horse race which is run at Aintree near Liverpool. Even people who don't usually gamble will place a bet on the Grand National. Sports are often combined

with gambling in England, and millions of dollars are bet each year especially on horse, greyhound, and pigeon races. About two out of every five adults fill in the football pools each week.

Team games
Soccer (the popular name for Association Football) attracts the largest number of spectators. All the professional soccer clubs have loyal supporters who watch them play regularly through the season from August to May. The highlights of the season are the Football Association Cup Final and the League Cup Final. Unfortunately a few soccer fans spoil the enjoyment for others through their hooliganism. English football supporters have gained a bad reputation both at home and abroad. Soccer is also a very popular participation sport. It's played in nearly all schools and there are thousands of amateur clubs that field teams each week. Although it has always been a male game in the past, many girls are now putting on their soccer boots, too.

Cricket is known as the English national game. Records show that it has been played since as far back as the 1550s. The rules of the game were established in the eighteenth century by the Marylebone Cricket Club, based at the world famous Lord's Cricket Ground in London. Most towns and villages have at least one cricket team. Over the past ten years more people have become interested in watching cricket and it is one of the nation's favorite summer sports. Professional county teams play in competitions and there are also several international matches during the year. The annual five-day Test matches are always

More and more people are taking up flying in one form or another! Hang gliding is very popular in areas with high open land, such as the Sussex Downs, and many a quiet Sunday has been disturbed by the drone of motorized hang gliders called microlites. Hot air balloons, gliders, and parachutes are now a fairly common sight over the English countryside.

well attended. These matches are played between England and a touring team from Australia, New Zealand, India, Pakistan, or the West Indies.

Rugby football is another game that was invented in England. It was first played in 1823 at Rugby School in Warwickshire and is named after the school. There are two types of rugby football, each with different rules. Rugby Union is played with 15 people to a side and is an amateur game. Rugby League is a 13 to a side game, played mainly in the North of England by both amateurs and professionals.

Sports old and new

For health conscious people, the new sport of the 1980s is jogging or running. Enthusiasts regularly run around the streets and parks and there are fun runs and marathon races in different places every weekend. A large number of people take part in the London Marathon and the Great North Run. People are also becoming much more interested in water sports. They are now trying their skills at windsurfing, scuba diving, and water skiing as well as the more usual swimming, sailing, and canoeing. The challenge of sports such as hang gliding, hot-air ballooning, and flying aircraft appeals to the adventurous. Other favorite outdoor sports are walking, salt or freshwater fishing, golf, athletics, cycling, and tennis.

Sports facilities and gyms provide for a wide variety of indoor sports and activities such as badminton, squash, bowling, exercising, yoga, gymnastics, and table tennis. Television coverage of "snooker," billiards, and darts championships has inspired people to try these games and they are now very popular. Volleyball, basketball, and American football have also recently gained a big following of fans who watch and play. Since the 1960s disabled people have taken part in sports and the first sports stadium in the world designed for disabled people was opened at Stoke Mandeville in 1969.

Vacations

Children and adults often go on sporting and activity vacations to learn something new or improve their skills. Some courses teach sports such as golf and badminton and leisure pursuits including crafts, photography, and other skills. Other courses cater to those who want more dangerous activities such as pot-holing, exploration of deep holes formed by wearing away of rock. The popular vacation season is from May to September but not everyone takes one. About a third of the people in England don't go on vacation at all. Of those that do, only a third go abroad; the rest prefer to stay in Great Britain.

English families like to go out just for the day. Country parks make a pleasant change from the dirt and fumes of the large towns and cities for walkers who enjoy the fresh air and natural surroundings. There are plenty of seaside resorts to visit as well. Among the traditional seaside towns are Blackpool, Southend, Brighton, Skegness, and Weston-Super-Mare. Over the past few years some of England's beaches have become very polluted, but there's been a campaign to clean them up. English people are renowned for their love of stately homes and gardens; they also like to go to the many museums. Safari and wildlife parks are attracting more and more visitors, and so are the recently built theme parks with their daredevil rides.

In the home
The English are fairly home-oriented, and many leisure activities are centered on the home. Nearly all households now have a television and on average people spend at least 20 hours a week watching programs. Nature documentaries and soap operas are both popular in England. One in three households now has a video cassette recorder so that the family can watch films or prerecorded television programs. Knitting, sewing, reading newspapers, magazines and books, listening to music and the radio, and entertaining friends are all ways of spending spare time.

Many people in England are enthusiastic gardeners. If their home doesn't have a garden, then they often fill window-boxes or pots with flowers. Dedicated gardeners can rent plots of land called allotments to grow vegetables and flowers. Do-it-yourself home improvement is now a popular hobby, and new superstores all over the country sell tools and other hardware, for jobs around the home. Many people are also very fond of animals and one household in two has a pet. Dogs and cats are the most common.

At the pub
The "public house" or tavern, is a traditional place for socializing, especially for men. About half of all adults spend at least one evening a week in the pub. Children under 14 are not allowed in pubs. In northern towns there are special clubs

Visiting historic houses and gardens is a very popular pastime in England. These gardens at Compton Acres, near Poole in Dorset, attract thousands of visitors each year. The interest in preserving these old buildings and gardens led to the formation of the National Trust, which acquires and looks after old houses and areas of natural beauty. Sometimes large properties are left to the National Trust when the owner dies.

called working men's clubs where entertainers often put on a cabaret act of singing or comedy. Young people may go to the cinema, night club, dance hall, or disco.

Restaurants serve a wide variety of different foods including French, Italian, Chinese, Greek, Indian, and American, and many people enjoy trying the foods of various countries. Far more prefer to pick up a "take out" fast food meal such as fish and chips (french fries) or Chinese food to eat at home.

English eating habits have changed over recent years. Cooked breakfasts and teatime spreads are almost a thing of the past. Most people have a light breakfast, a snack at lunchtime and then an evening meal which is often frozen from the supermarket. However, Sunday lunch is still important in England, when the whole family sits around the table to eat a cut of meat, vegetables, and roast potatoes.

10   From Shakespeare to Top of the Pops

For centuries music, dance, drama, painting, and literature have thrived in England, and English people possess a rich arts heritage.

One famous English writer is Charles Dickens who lived from 1812 until 1870. Dickens described, in his novels such as *Oliver Twist* and *The Pickwick Papers*, the lives of the people he saw around him in the nineteenth century. He often wrote about hardship and poverty, especially the overcrowded, dirty streets and homes in London. Dickens himself suffered poverty when his father was jailed for not paying his debts. Dickens was sent to work in a factory but he later used his unhappy experience to write *David Copperfield*.

Life was very different for novelist Jane Austen who lived from 1775 until 1817. She was the daughter of a clergyman and she lived a quiet, comfortable life. In her books, such as *Emma, Pride and Prejudice,* and *Persuasion,* Jane Austen described the lifestyles of the English middle classes during the eighteenth century.

William Shakespeare

Best-known of all the writers born in England is the poet and playwright, William Shakespeare. Shakespeare was born in 1564 in Stratford-upon-Avon and he probably attended the local grammar school there. He wrote many plays including *A Midsummer Night's Dream, King Lear, The Tempest, Hamlet, Richard III,* and *Macbeth.*

During his lifetime, plays were performed throughout England by touring groups of actors. In London, Shakespeare's plays were performed in the newly built Globe Theatre on the south bank of the Thames River. Today, over 400 years later, Shakespeare's plays are still regularly performed both in England and in many other countries all around the world. In Stratford, the Royal Shakespeare Theatre, which specializes in presenting plays written by Shakespeare, attracts thousands of theatergoers every year including many from overseas.

There are many theaters in England today. London alone has over 100, including about 40 in its famous West End area. The National Theatre is also in London, on the south bank of the Thames near where the Globe once stood. The National Theatre is really three theaters: The Cottesloe, the Lyttelton, and the Olivier. The Olivier is the biggest of the three theaters with seats for over 1,500 people. The National Theater has its own group of actors called the National Theatre Company. Another major theater in London is in the Barbican Complex. In fact, the Barbican has two stages. One stage is used for large-scale performances; the other, called the Pit, is used mainly for new plays. The Barbican also has a large concert hall that attracts famous musicians and conductors from around the world.

Opera and ballet

One of England's most well-known composers this century is Benjamin Britten. Britten was born in 1913 and while he was still very young be began to write music. Eventually, in 1948 he started the

England boasts several internationally known ballet companies. The leading ballet company is based at the Royal Opera House, Covent Garden, London. This photograph shows members of the company dancing in Still Life at the Penguin Café.

Aldeburgh Festival of Music, which still takes place every year. He wrote many songs and several operas including *Peter Grimes* and *Billy Budd*. Operas are very costly to present as they involve many people such as musicians, dancers, actors, designers, set-makers, costume-makers, makeup artists, and singers. This means that tickets for performances are usually expensive. The two main places to see opera in England are the Coliseum and the Royal Opera House which are both in London. The Coliseum and the Royal Opera House also present performances of ballet which can also be seen in other large cities in England.

Sometimes, mainly at Christmas and during the summer months, theaters put on special shows for children called pantomimes. Favorites include *Cinderella*, *Jack and the Beanstalk*, and *Babes in the Wood*. There's plenty of opportunity for children to hiss and boo at the "villains" and to call out advice to the "good guys," and there is always a happy ending!

Film

Both children and adults enjoy going to the movies. For a while it seemed that television might deter people from wanting to go to the movies since they could see films in their own homes, so many movie houses were shut or converted into bingo halls. However, people do enjoy going out to see a film and the movies are once again very popular. Films are graded U, PG, 15, and 18, according to who may see them. You

---

Dame Ninette de Valois is the founder of the Royal Ballet. She was born in Ireland in 1898, and her real name is Edris Stannus. In the days when she began dancing it was fashionable for all ballet dancers to adopt French or Russian names, for these countries had the most famous ballet companies. In the 1920s, Dame Ninette worked with Diaghilev in his Ballet Russes. In 1931, she founded her own company in England, together with the famous theater impresario Lillian Baylis. This was called Sadler's Wells Ballet, until it became the Royal Ballet in 1956. Dame Ninette built up a wide selection of classical and modern ballets for her company, and also created her own ballets, such as *The Rake's Progress* and *Checkmate*. The huge success of the Royal Ballet is largely due to her determination and dedication.

may not see a film marked 18 until you are over 18 years old. Films are shown in the afternoon and in the evening. Some excellent films have been made in England and there is a highly respected movie industry.

Pop music

For young people a major art form is pop music, although many older people do not have the same tastes. All across England, groups of young people get together in bedrooms, garages, and sometimes halls to form groups and make music. Rock concerts are usually very well attended. Many are held at Wembley where thousands of people will fill the arena for a popular group. Many people listen to the radio to hear the latest pop sounds. The longest running pop music show on television is BBC 1's Top of the Pops which is presented by two radio disc jockeys and has been broadcast since the early 1960s. The most well-known of all English pop groups is still the Beatles who first became famous during the 1960s with songs such as "Strawberry Fields," "Penny Lane," and the conceptual album *Sgt. Peppers Lonely Hearts Club Band.*

Art

The cover of the Beatle's album *Sgt. Pepper* was designed by the artist Peter Blake. Examples of Peter Blake's painting can be seen hanging in the Tate Gallery in London. A second Tate Gallery has recently been opened in Liverpool. In all, there are over 1,500 public galleries and museums in England. Famous English painters from the past include Constable, Gainsborough, and Turner.

Lawrence Stephen Lowry was born in 1887 and worked as a clerk, painting only in his spare time until he retired at 65. He died in 1976. He created pictures peopled with matchstick men and women. They were very simple but beautiful paintings and made an excellent record of the industrial area in which he lived. His paintings have become very popular among collectors.

John Constable is perhaps the most widely known of English painters. He lived from 1776 to 1837 and is famous for his landscape pictures particularly of the area where he was born, East Bergholt in Suffolk. his father was a miller, and copies of Constable's painting of the mill are seen in many English homes. His paintings are notable for showing many sides of the ever-changing English weather! His other well-known paintings are of Salisbury Cathedral, Hampstead, Dedham Vale, and one titled *The Leaping Horse* (1825). He became a member of the Royal Academy in 1829 and his painting *The Haywain* won a medal in France, where he was very popular.

Henry Moore was one of England's leading sculptors. He and his friend Barbara Hepworth were among the leaders of the movement into modern sculptural forms in England. These large sculptures are in Hyde Park, London. The bronze in the foreground reflects Moore's interest in the "reclining figure."

One painter, L.S. Lowry, lived quietly in Salford all his life. Salford is an industrial town in the north of England, and Lowry recorded the industrial scenes and people he saw every day. The English sculptor Henry Moore is world famous. Like Lowry, Moore was born in the north of England. He made sculptures in wood, stone, and bronze, many of them based either on the human form or on shapes Moore had seen in nature. Sculptures by Moore can be seen in art galleries and public places throughout England and the world.

Index